Decoding Samara

Patrick Deeley

DEDALUS

The Dedalus Press
24 The Heath ~ Cypress Downs ~ Dublin 6W
Ireland

Cover Painting by Renate Braun

ISBN 1 901233 55 3 (paper)
ISBN 1 901233 56 1 (bound)

Acknowledgements:

to — *Cyphers; The Irish Times; Atlanta Review; Poetry Canada; The Literary Review; Chapman; Poetry Ireland Review; Stream And Gliding Sun; A Wicklow Anthology; Wildeside; The Stinging Fly; Books Ireland; The Shop* — where some of these poems were published.

Dedalus Press books are represented and distributed in the U.S.A. and Canada by **Dufour Editions Ltd.**, P.O. Box 7, Chester Springs, Pennsylvania 19425
in the UK by **Central Books**, 99 Wallis Road, London E9 5LN

The Dedalus Press receives financial assistance from
An Chomhairle Ealaíon, The Arts Council, Ireland.
Printed in Dublin by Colour Books Ltd

for
Judy, Alan & Genevieve

and for
Ena, Simon, Bridie and Vincent

Contents

Rathgar Pastoral	9
Hornets' Nest	10
Instrument	11
Willow Pattern	12
Domestic Hitch	13
Tree Genius	14
Tree House	15
Dargle Oak	16
Taina's Evocations	17
Flood River	18
Heron	19
To The Dryad	20
Tableau	21
Worship	22
Testament	23
For A Gardener	24
Pollarded Beech	25
Codling Moth Larvae	27
Understandable Gap	28
Impatiens	29
Elegy	30
By Cruagh Wood	31
Evergreen	32
The Cot	33

King Of The Wood	36
Yard Sticks	37
Sap Myth	38
The Workbench	40
Eclipse	41
Red Sash	42
Panache	43
In Killalaghton Churchyard	45
First Fruits	47
Legend	48
The Antique King	49
Críochán Thorn	51
Burren	52
Names Remain	53
The Dissatisfied Youth	54
Son Of Hazel	56
Cromlach's Deception	58
The King Of South Galway	60
Baile And Aillinn	62
Ash	63

Rathgar Pastoral

Half a century, maybe more, ago,
a Rathgar woman kept a cow
which she stabled nightly
on ground we now call garden.

What was then open country
is all but inner suburb;
swallowed, too, the calp quarry
and its overspilling lake.

A lone windmill, deployed
to drain the lake, whirls again
in a story told at bedtime
to set our children dreaming.

The quarry cow slips our minds.
She wanders off to graze
the spaces between strewn
boulders where grass glistens.

The woman is unconcerned.
She ambles into the setting sun,
just away from our sapling
Victoria plum, which is opening out

in blossom. Casually as my
mother might, she reaches down
for her milking bucket,
and starts to rattle its handle.

Hornets' Nest

A paper lampshade, but many times
layered, at the tip of whose
warm, plump cone no bulb peeps,
only a small black aperture
designed for entrance and exit.

The flat base is glued, not hung,
above our heads, in a corner
of the boilerhouse. Summer gave us
no reason to potter here. Now
we are too late to see the hornets.

But taking heart from wonders
which the world (if it ever stops
to think about them at all)
might call insignificant —
earthworms gowned in a froth

of mating, earwigs nestling
their young, or those grasshoppers
we met in a Wicklow glen,
hosts unwary enough to allow us
touch off them — we cherish

the elaborate, empty nest,
the notion of a lampshade wrought
from regurgitated tree-bark,
flowers, sap; we envision nature's
living lights ranged forever out.

INSTRUMENT

It could function both
as pen-holder and paperweight,
this raft of tubes
moulded together and glazed
smooth to the touch.

Mostly I let it idle.
But once, looking out at the green
swirl of a tree
tousled by summer squall,
freshly budded leaves

plucked and tossed,
I thought of how the goat god
pestered the nymph
with his amorous attentions —
(she escaped

literally into the ground,
to emerge again
a reed) — and then this came to me
as mouthable in a way
that words aren't,

as something I might blow
through to eloquence
beyond words, until even the tune
itself must fade,
stilling ode and elegy.

Willow Pattern

Chinese pagodas burgeon
as unlikely branches
bearing implausible fruits,
banners of wheat blow,
and two bluebirds curve
forever towards a kiss

in double-four array.
Working around the stock
emblems of plenitude
and happiness, we find
they still hold good,
twelve years after

our dresser's coronation.
Turn. Take another look.
The soda bread slowly cools,
the apples and oranges
(eat a day, a day replenish)
fulfil us in their bowl.

Domestic Hitch

Tiny crest-and-trough indicator
comes on green, but the tumbler
won't turn. Machine's temperamental,
your clothes and mine, lumped
together behind its roundy window,
buttonhole us here, fresh out
of storm, who promised each other
the given afternoon. But press
the window, love, lean barefoot
back beside me in our ample chair
and press; thigh tensing thigh,
we'll coax the window gently,
gently click into lost automatic.

Tree Genius

We pass the days of your infant leisure
under this cedar, the Cedar of Lebanon,
high summer ranges round and round
the gargantuan bole. Your head peeps,
your laughter floats upward and meshes
with the intricate needlework of leaves.
Storeyed branches so spread and feed
the tree's sense of its own place
that I must lift you over my shoulders
to give perspective. You grow still,
your mind turns dendritic, mapping these
adroit windows and chambers of space.

TREE HOUSE

The attic's converted; the dust
has settled. That potential
for darkness or deluge which we knew
was waiting always, held

in haphazard abeyance above us,
still is, though veneered now
with bright surfaces. And a store
of airy notions roosts high up,

far back in our heads,
a tree house springs to mind.
Engage a chair. The sun will come
round by afternoon to your way

of thinking. Birdsong will be
an uncomplicated friend. The moon
will please herself. And as
we lift from wishing you

goodnight, the framed stars — extant
against a city sky's rapturous
brushstrokes of indigo and orange —
will pierce our hearts with love.

Dargle Oak

A forgotten thermos flask,
stuck under the oxter
of the fallen oak. Which is
itself all but forgotten,

the god fallen, with one
intact arm jutting
out of this hillside. Root
below the mossy coverlet,

clay bark and mouldy wood
tuft to hand. A white grub
with an orange-capped head
plays dead. But here

is a sheltered surprise,
mere ghost of a green
chance, oak-leaf sprig-god,
redemptive, yet to rise.

TAINA'S EVOCATIONS

Then this letter lands, its envelope
archipelagoes astir in aqua-marine, or,
looked at again, sky through cirrus,
but however I angle or edge it, a map
of endeavours made by a woman
who retains the use of only one hand.
When days attempting 'the big look'
leave me vacant, and every resource
is drying up, I will open afresh
and hold before me Taina's evocations —
of peat bogs and conifers, and auroras
bedazzling icy lakes. Such tawny stains,
such swirls and swims, I must take
on trust the thin-skinned tremblings
of my plain of mosses, callows, fens.

Flood River

She's wild again — Dodder indeed!
She's washing the brown hills
down. For merriment she will spin
the wheels of a discarded pram.

And for a change, she will woo
the willows. She'll put a stop
to lower-road traffic. Tar-nation
and cars, she's slipping boundaries

we set her, spilling over them.
Our collie hears her before we can.
He roves on ahead — his own
meanderer. He will come back

in a while, shaking wet to tell us
the park is a pond. Mallard
circle it. And when we get there,
seems even the stone seats float.

HERON

By the haze of a streetlight we make you out,
shanked in shallows near the Dodder's
far bank, with your tail to the trees
and your eye on us. Heron, said by farmers
to harbinger Spring, here on St Stephen's Night!
Shy wetlander, our settling suburbanite!
Some day — for no reason other than that we
met you, and spoke across the divide,
and that, however strange or preposterous
it seems, you replied — one of us will draw
this ramble down, let it orient thought
away from path and parapet, and all
appurtenance designed to set us straight.
There in reverie we will again watch you
go, sweep emphatic — head low, neck tucked
into shoulders — upriver, through the airflow.

To The Dryad

The besiegements of winter lift.
Not as cloud, and not as my tilt
at these perennial ivy clusters
sporting on high their black berries
and their top-heavy tangle. But lift

in the way the tree strikes me
differently — as airings of your shimmy
up where branches leaf themselves
afresh, elbowing, occluding
the world I know. My climb is less

a far-fetched fancy than the need
to sit loose-legged amid your canopy,
crowned by sun, holding the imprimatur
of a clear sky in my hand.
Below me, the villagers move

by earthly weights and measures,
certifying with seed and fertilizer
how and why their gardens grow.
I call by names they pleased to call you
long ago: dryad, green-blood, god.

They ask if you tap your head, or smile
sideways, or show yourself
to the tree. But what throws me — they
fall silent now — is the burst of a dove
from your branches, thunderously.

Tableau

(In some places the people worried about how the beams of wood that went towards the making of a house might be planted — not for fear the house might fall, but because they wanted the dryad or hamadryad that dwelled in the timber, to stay upsides with the world.)

If a tree spirit resides among our kitchen
planks of pine, he must lie lengthwise,
holding the blond grains tight about him,
robes to hide behind, and these dark knots
we may suppose are shades he wears
against the sun. No chirp from him — full
up, thirst slaked on spilt tea, his ribs
tickled with an airy cloth! No evidence.
But then, he'd be a fool to show. We'd have
to throw him out. He'd not make wilderness.

Worship

Forest and cathedral in common hold
a hush to stillness. Let the visitation
be of one or a handful of pilgrims,
spiritual crux is coaxed to resolve.
Where pagan shouted *coill*, a wood,
and priest insisted *cill*, a church,
our placenames remember *Kilmore, Kylemore* —
but whether they intend *The Big Wood* or
The Big Church is unclear, and we
needn't incline to draw a distinction.

Testament

Taking my cue from Pentateuch,
I figured life as a tree.
So that it became less a case
of deluge than of Noah
crafting his ark from gopher wood.

Nor was it God's covenant
with the earth, recast by rainbow
(come abatement, come the dove),
held me to any detail other
than that the twig was olive.

What stick did Moses strike
against the rock? Surely hazel,
by which my father divined
a well. And manna offered
food for thought: had it blown

from flowering ash, or was it
fungal? There I fell back
on Solomon raising — so it would
endure after he had gone —
his temple of Cedar of Lebanon.

For A Gardener

Then I stood acquainted
with the Lady Chapel
hid in the side of St Joseph's,
and caught the silence
tumbling in splinters

of stained glass light
from two windows painted
by Harry Clarke.
My eye fell full
on *Our Lady Queen of Heaven*

in Glory. Not the form
alone, more the colours
emanating — green, gold,
lemon, blue — all
among the Biblical women,

all a bower I would bring
alive here, spade
by hour, my climbing
season come, my bench mark
clay, sun and shower.

Pollarded Beech

I still call you *queen*,
although you lost your head
years ago to a forester
who turned firewood squire,

cropping off the bough.
He so forced you to bear
the absence of true branches
that you must squat

and swell, holding the gists
of grand leafy lofts
down to make solid
as dead heartwood, as gnarl.

Yet no containment's
possible. You fiercely attempt
the old crowning grace,
you sprout at weird angles,

in rods and shoots, frazzles
and tangles, in splinters
almost, but for the mending
glove of your skin.

I still call you regal,
overlooking your grotesques —
a wood-knitted owl's face,
and a rat's — with fractal

calculations of leaf
and limb, with manifold twists
coalesced in an aerial pool
where you catch the sun.

CODLING MOTH LARVAE

Their webbed nest has tucked
and folded the apple leaves
in, over, around. Rain runs off,
glistering the gauze; wind
won't blow such a house down.

But when leaves fall sallow,
in a day or two, the larvae
swing to some new twig,
well away. All of one suit,
one gullet, they nod and wag,

soft egalitarians amid
succulence. To a point where I
pinch their entire construct
neatly out, and peer through
its slow sunder between my hands.

A ticklish effect. They rub
themselves, slip the quake
of leaf and silk. I puppeteer
unseen stringlets, raise
and lower my laconic regrets.

Understandable Gap

Simeon the stylite,
if I could go
back to your century,
I'd want to know

why you live in a tree.
And you, no doubt,
would ask about
the tree living in me.

Impatiens

The busy Lizzie Thomas brought in
would never amount to much, its soft
stems broken at the elbows,
but such was the ceremony with which
he presented it, I made room
among the conkers, cones, acorns.

Soon we returned to the graft
of sums and spellings. A box of chalks
had worn out before either of us
thought again to pass remarks
on impatiens. (My composure had withered
in face of the riddles his mind

posed. Thwarted by abacus
but not coin. Spelling *sing* for *sign*,
yet an able tracker of fox and rabbit.)
And the plant had proved me
wrong. All branchy now, a leafy spill
down the cracked plastic pot.

Come Spring, it blossomed, pale
pink asterisks, and Thomas decided
it might be better off in his caravan.
He, too, had gone before June,
head shaking: "See, I served my time;
I've roads, not books, to travel."

Elegy

Surmounting the ordinary flatness,
a lios. Streamlet runs-in-wait,
laughs me out of it. The further
I go, the more appreciably distance
greens. The man I saw making hay
last August is dying in a near
cottage. Neighbour, what can I say
to suddenness, streamlet, lios,
to the lurch of a big yellow frog
across my boot? Only that our road
ran through summer, its children
already tall as we were, you swore,
"Jez, there must be new methods
of making them," then we scanned
afar the blue apparition of hills.

By Cruagh Wood

Not wasp but sawfly, alighted
on bark, spearing its sharp ovipositor
deep into this pine tree.

The egg will hatch, grub blindly,
take years to make a return journey.
The pine will shed golden tears —

which are really viscous traps
against attack. Call these *resin*,
each dissipating a tiny cloud

of turpentine. And if commerce bleed
a host of angled cuts
into hanging pots, let the bark

be *blaze*. The tree necessarily goes
along with this. But left
to nature, it may lock

an insect in an amber bead,
to be discovered by a child
as yet unborn, and held for silhouette

against the bevel
of a wonder-blown eye, the admirable
light of a Dublin Mountain day.

Evergreen

Clay colours slipping off the cliff-face
above us, pine trees collapsing
in various 'states of stagger'
between two extremes — a gentle

incline for some which stand
farthest back, a grassy bind-and-gag
tightening around others
already given to this dell

where we lie lazing on skeins
of dead heather and fern. Weatherings
roll mud drops out between
the roots of those next bound

for the abyss. But falling or floored,
all still hold onto evergreen,
delaying their doom and the moment
when we rise away from them.

The Cot

Since it went eventually down
to dream amid my townlands
of Addergoole and Lurgan,

I must stop and suppose
a great-great-grandfather's
great-grandfather, felling

and hollowing Ireland's
hugest oak, fashioning a crude
canoe, a communal row-boat:

fog-breaths of ferried cattle
occlude its every twist,
cargoes of lumber and chat

draw close to home.
The lank-boned paddlers come,
each with my thin face,

mine and my father's hawk-nose —
as if blood had clanned
such traits in all of us.

Calmly they size me up;
teeth whet old saws
familiar to my childhood: "Always

work the dry hour. Turn ever
only the bright side out."
While this cot, their craft,

so long sunk in obsolescence
and so well preserved,
floats and flexes them all

in favours passing for more
than figment or silhouette.
No answer can I make before

they again go, adrift
in reeds, aground in bog clay,
their legend a buried artefact

full of forgotten rudiments,
their endeavour expended
unavailingly — although

the river still wends its way,
the blood perseveres in me.
And I am sternly alone,

telling myself their calluses
have turned to snail-shells,
their ribs wrestle blackthorns

round by Addergoole,
their shrunken skulls
are mushrooms springing still.

King Of The Wood

Winter egg-breakfasts. We saved
the shells to helmet twigs of Spring.
Which was a whitethorn tree,
buttered and creamed with primroses

from the ditches, and danced around.
Our childhood, if we but knew,
a wilding dolled up in pagan ritual,
a throaty echo of the barbarian's

lost hurrah. He threw shapes
with us there, our woodman father,
stubble on his chin and sawdust
in his hair. His old credulousness

from before the calendared moon,
the unreliable sun configurated
to clock, had been gradually tempered
to a gentle wisdom. He became

tranquil as the wood, his speech
so many silver-grey ash trunks
stealing upward to leaf-canopies
of interlinking boughs. In his face,

the sun's luminosity was occluded
now, now a sparring opulence.
Once, he lifted a hand to shade
my eyes, and it grew green-blooded.

Yard Sticks

Stepping the felled tree was a balancing act
I often tried in ash woods of childhood.
Branches gave trampolines. Or where they
jutted stoutly upward, climbing poles.

And when the bole began to roller, I leaped.
But each tree implied furniture. Lopped
of its limbs, trailered to the mill, it became
a series of planks and yard sticks.

If I twigged to aesthetics of leaf or bird,
or to the gap in morning a downed tree makes,
there they still were — yard sticks —
stacked for the carpenter's apprentice.

Slide rule, set-square, found my measure.
But when, one day, I shelved a pencil
behind my ear, blood and imagery whispered to
each other, slowly decoding *samara*, the keys.

Sap Myth

The Basoga tribesman on TV
knelt and sipped from the axe-cut
which he had sunk in a tree.

Was it respect, or an old
curiosity concerning the taste,
dipped his head, I wondered,

or a humour of his forefathers
honoured. He never uttered a word,
the move was swiftly made,

the camera momentarily eluded.
A commentator interpreted
this mouthing of sap to signify

brotherhood — tree man, man tree —
but afterwards in local
Ballyduggan woods, I sank an axe

and felt the story come to me
purely and simply as a cure
for thirst! Bittersweet, intimate,

though I cannot say a green
god's blood had claimed my tongue
only to free it. Nor say —

even if my tenderest lyric grow
from a tree — that sap I drank
in childhood gave the air to me.

The Workbench

Countless hammer-blows struck,
axe chippings, scrape-marks
of saw, vice-grip indentations,
plane and chisel scars, burrowings
made by bit and nail.

How many of these dealings
were intentional? Few, I'd say.
Should we put them down to slippage, then,
miscalculation, failure of the eye
to find its vision?

When you set to work, each
hand-made implement falling
fractions short of machine-won
finesse, I recognise the beauty
of little blemishes:

the finished article comes fresh
and distinct, drawing
an antique's endearments. And indeed
there are welts, reboundings
off the tasks.

But the workbench is stout enough
to take them all, to absorb
and wear the hardship, so further
particularising itself, through each
new thing you shape.

Eclipse

1

The missing segment of a grindstone
which broke while I was working it
in our carpentry shop, comes to mind
as an exact fit for this covered portion
of moon — momentarily — before
a further slip towards total eclipse.

2

Why should I think it incredible
that the ancients hurled their spears
moonward, in anger at her dying?
Haven't I seen you under a big shade,
sensible, courteous, tendering
regrets to the trees you must fell?

Red Sash

Wearing plaid, wearing short, heavy-duty jackets
and steel-caulked boots — train-wreckers,
corduroy-pavers, revvers of chainsaws, wisecracking
descendants of the Red Sash. I saw them
in a film, wintering under bark. I heard tell
from your brother who'd been to Northern California
and back. (I'd not gone when he asked.)

Our sawmill tested me, and I the lumberjack myth —
in Galway woods. The blade's haranguing journey
through each ash, opened a gap in my beliefs.
And after you had died, *at stump*, as they might say,
I thought of how the film grew quiet,
of how they untied a dead companion's boots
to hang by the laces on a tree standing nearest.

Makeshift commemoration, I suppose,
the best that rough and ready lives could manage,
but this gesture I kept clear of timber
because you were my father still and for always —
smiling, unbroken, on the go — in memories
borne beyond the pitiless incidentals of a chipped
fingernail, a foxglove sprouted at your temple.

PANACHE

Your face has vanished
from our sky. (And did you never
turn on us a kindly eye?)
Your bellow is blown
beyond cajole. Your patrol —
which must have been

distinctive — is untraceable.
Even your labours
decline you in their redundancy.
Who will make hay
as you did? Who deploy
scythe or breast-sleán now?

Nobody. And nobody
is sorry. The long-handled
back-breakers you lived by
hang from wall-laths,
rusting. Your haggard's
a weed-embroidered museum.

Yet if I could compose poetry
the way you shook barley —
those seed-pellets
syllables, that bucket
a headful of shifting nuance —
my lines would swerve

and hop, I'd cast the words
precisely, with panache,
my hand opening a blessing
to the winds I'd know
were coming, that they might not
lodge but let me sway.

In Killalaghton Churchyard

Only scraps of the old stories
stay, yet sufficient
to show how full of enchantments
nature stood, long ago.

One woman saw the bare stick
which she had leaned on
in hardship, blossom
with a sudden change of luck.

Another envisioned a tree
branching from her own neck,
and the dream foretold
she would found a dunasty.

Whether by saint or pagan
moved, the earth bequeathed
good. Or, having its favourites
fall, the earth bedevilled.

With Patrick's religion winning
a fervent multitude,
tenacious, snag-sinewed gods
clung beneath the whirr

of blessing and miracle.
It took famine to break that grip
fully. The woebegone,
thinly crying towards heaven,

pushed clay away in their dying
into the now-despised
ground. A story still is told —
of a woman and child

who came seeking rest
from the hunger, and died here
in Kallalaghton Churchyard.
This ash tree is said to mark

their grave, its roots
bedded in the clayed forms,
turning every last vestige
into itself. Glancing afresh,

we see it's far too young.
And dismiss the folktale.
And yet find ourselves sparing
a thought, because the tree

occurs to us now as a prayer —
by seasons green against
each death, or cold
and bare, staying serenely put.

First Fruits

The gloom-bruised sloe,
bitter to its pith,
crinkled my palate
and bore me a squint.

The ditch-bound briar
tendered me to eat
each black multi-berry
as a dimpled shine.

The happy-looking haw
with lacquer glossing
mere bland as mellow
I always only skinned.

The golden crab apple —
farthest, loftiest —
was a legend raided
and a disappointment.

Legend

Autochthon, first native, self-birthed
or sprung from the earth, imagine
as the source of our musks and atavisms,
hugely possessive and possessed
of his place. Him the clean-cut hero —
the man with a vision — kills.
(Footprinting in pave his faded spoor
for tourists, floating a shopping mall
down to his broken lair.) Him
the townspeople never afterwards expect
to erupt in their dreams. And nature,
nature's the decapitated dragon
which yet again will regenerate —
a root, a thicket perhaps, a secret
forest let in some suburbanite's thought.

THE ANTIQUE KING

1

He is lowliest of the underwood,
making food as Sulphur Tuft
does, sparsely, from old tree-stump
and fallen log that has decayed.

He worships below the picture,
keeps one eye on the cathedral crux
of canopy, branch and bole.
He suffers shadow, then the clear

upturn and spiral into leaf.
He gathers gnarl, draws on dapple,
sounds and renders the wood
afresh to itself as his own word.

2

Let me follow his rolling realm,
dream those hills and villages
he paced before the first
rumblings of the wheel were heard —

a strict pastoral, where good
repute depends on word of growth.
The people make demands — his magic
responds, pushing the sun

up, the sappy stalk, the crops.
Let me catch his laugh — now —
while the wide, credulous world's
under his spreading hands.

3

He will be cautioned by witherings
of leaves and by their fall,
though these verdant canopies
are yet his cloak. Of a day

put out to shiver next the shorn
winter-blasted trees, he will
learn at his leisure that magic's
a falderal, and power a fluent

draining of the god by his
mortal body, and pride disposable.
So, laid low, he must huddle,
become another endangered species.

CRÍOCHÁN THORN

Was it three or four hawthorns
he had uprooted, the man who could
muster neither arm nor leg,
when he tried to rise next morning

from his bed? And what became
the character found darting
between two bushes, unable to decide
which he should fell first?

If the folk mind's a landscape,
you stand *mounded*, Críochán Thorn
of the Slieve Blooms, bidding me
keep my distance. And I do,

but with a grumbled word or two,
a little mocking gesture made
about your crookedness. For I know
the shape of malevolence was

never yours, just a scare you threw
across the moonlight, just
a shadow grafted to the thoughts
of people fumbling for a way

that might leave them unmolested.
And if the ruse has helped
to protect you, keep it — keep it so.
But, tell me about the man who ...

Burren

If I quicken here at all,
I stumble; if I stand still,
glares and glints
of reflected sunlight
make the white rocks
appear to alter and move.

My walkabout dreams up
a bubbling puddle
to enthuse the turlough,
dissipates tepid water
through rockery cups —
earth, vessel of vessels,

turns tipsy on scents
of wildflower, is cracked
about the clutchings
of tiny, ancient trees,
growing horizontally
in grikes below my feet.

Names Remain

Even the hard-headed landlords
could come up with a poetic turn,
proclaiming trees "the feathers
of the scape", yet next breath prepared
to pluck them as "an excrescence
of nature for the payment

of debts". Or as "a shelter
for all ill-disposed". Names remain —
Aharlogh, Dromfynine, Glanmore,
Glanflesk, Glangarrif, Glanrought,
Leanmore, Kilmore, Muskryquirke,
Kilhuggy, Glenglas, Glenconkeyn —

names that dip and sway, creak
and sough, beckoning us back, somehow,
to the broadleaf groves, the last
wildwoods, through syllables which
hold their music still, though they
are twisted out of the original.

The Dissatisfied Youth

(From a legend)

I keep to instructions.
Choose a wand from the willow,
carve it to a quadrangular figure,
and place it over the lintel
of my parents' door.

The house remains dead.
Long faces abide, bodies sit
unbudgeable. No conversation
and no kick from anyone, no leeway
given, nothing mooted

that's new or different or
for fun. The only moves are mine —
a whirl of angers, stomps,
gesticulations — all my steps misled
by the dance-maker's tune.

I throw the willow figure back,
its surfaces scored with the exact
runic spells he gave.
I pronounce him fake,
demand a refund. His response?

That there's no compassing
these mysteries. They misfire, being
whimsical, otherworldly, of trees,
and we yet learn something.
It’s time I should leave home.

Son Of Hazel

Finnéigeas tells him the sources
of the seven great rivers
are wells, and that nine hazel trees
overlook these — the nine
trees of knowledge. He describes

how the hazelnuts shake free,
singly, intermittently, through the good
graces of so many sunbeams,
raindrops and ripening winds.
"Each makes a little plop," he says,

"surprising the quiet places;
each moves on mystic bubbles,
inspiring even the fishes!" Finnéigeas,
old poet, vows to catch one such
hazelnut if he is spared the eye.

The youngster takes him with a grain
of salt. Mimics his mincing steps
as he comes and goes. Stoops
to tediously mesh and mend
his own fishing nets, to treat them

with birch-dye preservative. Whistles
until the day when a hazelnut's
gulped by a salmon, which carries
the knowledge on to where
Finnéigeas hauls it from the Boyne.

Then whistles again. Is thrown to tend
the smoking stippler on a spit.
There the blister rises,
impulsively he thumbs it, tastes
his burning thumb — whereupon

the super power is fired in him.
Mac Cúil, Son of Hazel, sees the future
unblurring. All atom and essence
slip within his ken. He sets
his heart on a saga of harnessings.

Cromlach's Deception

(From a 6th Century legend)

That my fingers and toes,
the chewed leaves and lobes
of my leprous ears,
my tongue and nose,
might grow pristine again,
again be whistling clean,
I wash in the River Shannon.

Little good its splash,
and less ease. Then
the sainted relics from Europe
strike me as piquant —
I quietly bundle them
into the great hollow elm
here at Clonmacnoise,

and wait up for morning.
Patrick would surely smirk,
pronounce my self-love
vain. I say bad cess to him!
But come dawn, all I know
is pain. The elm withholds
my potential salve,

it has swallowed and sealed
everything! When axe
strikes, woodchips fly
back into place. Dust
from my buckling cross-cut
again turns whole. I'm
bested by a pagan miracle.

THE KING OF SOUTH GALWAY

Ask and I gave. That was
my weakness, a refusal
to refuse. That was my strength
in the beginning. Hat, coat,

veritable shirt off my back.
And as I gave — ewe, cow, horse —
word went wildfire:
criticisms, esteems. Neither

did me good. Who would be
sainted alive and stay
level? Who would be classed
a glory-hound by some, by others

plain mad, and keep his cool?
I walked the shores
of this big lake, this bulge
in the Shannon, and cried

to nature for solace,
for avarice even, for the stints
and generosities by which
my neighbours live. I might

as well have been a kingfisher
nesting in the rib
of a river. Or an otter ruddering —
fluid's own incarnate —

to whom the gods permit
no alternative. “Your eyes,”
said the sly man who had come
from a long way off,

smiling, sniffing out the legend.
“Give me your eyes.”
And I twisted against these
fingers glutching the round

gristled pain of it all.
Down demented here to wash
I go, the lake wells up
about me, reddening —

‘his wound's reflection,’ people
say, and their Gaelic
clears it as *Dearg*, Lough *Derg*,
the sight I gave away.

Baile and Aillinn

He was coming south to court her,
she, making north to meet him,
when the false words of a stranger
who visited one, then the other,
lamenting to each, *your love is dead*,
broke their credulous hearts

and coldly accomplished what he said.
A yew tree shaded Baile's grave,
an apple tree dappled Aillinn's.
Here the story might have ended —
with his face arboreally remembered,
and hers transmogrifying branches.

Except that the poets of Ulster
decided one morning to carve the yew
into a tablet for their verses,
while the Leinster poets likewise
ear-marked the apple bole. At Tara,
Cormac mac Airt heard the poets

declaim. He settled the tablets,
one at either hand, with regal tact.
Whereupon they fabulously leaped
into each other — grains, metaphors,
calligraphies, twining and fusing
in an apotheosis of the love act.

Ash

Whether 'Excelsior Fraximus'
or 'Venus of the Woods',
you were once the *Big Bell*
of Borrisokane, whose twigs
and branches no-one dared burn —
in thrall to a legend
that they'd fire the house!

Talk of Kells, the scenario's
different. You genuflected
above St Keenan's Well,
and promptly bled — a miracle
so much more believable
than red-rotted vegetation,
in the eyes of the multitude.

And you were a tree at Killura
made sacred to Craebhnat,
which emigrants plucked
on their way to the ships —
a charm against drowning,
if not starvation — until soon
no trace of you stood.

But shush! Let scholars
glossing each name and fame
lay claim to the tree
they know. You dwell in us
simply as ash, you raise
from the plain gifts intended
for our silence, our eyes.